APPALACHIAN MOUNTAINS

APPALACHIAN MOUNTAINS

BY CLYDE H. SMITH

TEXT BY WILMA DYKEMAN and DYKEMAN STOKELY

International Standard Book Number 0-912856-59-9
Library of Congress Catalog Number 80-65134
Copyright© 1980 by Graphic Arts Center Publishing Co.
P.O. Box 10306 • Portland, Oregon 97210 • 503/224-7777
Publisher • Charles H. Belding
Designer • Robert Reynolds
Printer • Graphic Arts Center
Binding • Lincoln & Allen
Printed in the United States of America

Lone tamarack (frequently called larch) emits a burst of autumn's color along the Allagash Waterway in northern Maine.

Hikers view sunset from summit of 4,393 foot Mt. Mansfield highest point in Vermont. Left: Buildings clustered on summit of 6,288 foot Mt. Washington, denote size of this mighty cone. Situated in White Mountains of New Hampshire it is highest peak in the northeast. Pages 8 and 9 following: Sunlight adds brilliant color to snow covered plain in upper New York.

Dawn breaks over Vermont's Camels Hump first seen by early French explorers from Lake Champlain. Right: Queen Anne's lace (wild carrot), daisies, clover and black-eyed susans form blanket of wild-flowers in Virginia. Pages 12 and 13 following: Virgin forests of Great Smoky Mountains apear endless, looking west from North Carolina border at Newfound Gap.

Harvest moon from summit of
4,784 foot Brasstown Bald,
highest elevation in Georgia.
Left: Desoto Falls in Little River
Canyon, example of rugged
terrain near southern tip of
Appalachian chain, where it
merges with rolling hills of
Alabama.

APPALACHIAN MOUNTAINS

Rain shrouds the rough dark trunks of oak and hickory trees, the gnarled sourwood, the crumbling chestnut stump, splatters gently onto the leathery leaves of rhododendron clustered along the hillside, drips through lacy webs of ferns and clumps of burnished bronze and green galax leaves to sink through centuries-old layers of mulch into underground capillaries and hidden rivulets, gather through the veins of Beaverdam Creek and the French Broad River into the mighty arteries of the Tennessee, and Ohio and the Mississippi and finally merge with the gulf and seas where it was born.

In childhood it was good to lie awake at night and eavesdrop on the water sinking into the great sponge of forest topsoil, splashing over the humpbacked stones in the rushing creek. Smell of the rain on acid leaf-mulch was fresh and faintly bitter. In these Blue Ridge highlands a thousand and more miles from the Maine woods a person could be drenched in the same raw primordial mists that Thoreau called "a damp and intricate wilderness, the fresh and natural surface of the planet." We were linked to Thoreau by the long green chain of the Appalachian Mountains.

It was also good to leave our home cupped among steep wooded slopes and drive north to visit another ancestral homeland in the spacious Hudson River country. Here and farther north in New England where there were visits to be made the landscape was familiar—but different. At the wind-whipped summit of Mt. Washington waited a cold desert of ancient boulders, a stark contrast to Mt. Mitchell not far from our North Carolina home, whose 6,684 feet (2,039 meters) made it the highest mountain in the entire Appalachian system and all of eastern America but whose evergreen crest of dark spruce forest made it seem gentler, more accessible than its northern counterpart. There were other differences. In the north we discovered lakes and ponds scattered like prodigal gems gleaming among hills and valleys. In the southern mountains where the land was never gouged by glaciers there was less quiet water, more sparkling springs and flashing streams.

This dual heritage brought singular awareness of the Appalachians at their innermost fold of leaf and stone and in the unravelling of their complex system of peaks and valleys down the spine of eastern America. These mountains demand and deserve knowledge carried to the bone. And the more that is known the more there is to know for the Appalachian Mountains—a domain larger than Great Britain—remain a land of paradox and a continuing frontier.

From the days of the Indians who fashioned myths to "explain" the mountains to the present moment when geologists are reexamining scientific evidence of their own explanations, there has been unanimous recognition of two Appalachian features: first, the rich variety of life in these mountains and second, the sense that nothing in them is separate from the whole. Tender filaments of trailing arbutus roots, dark treasures of coal locked below the surface of the earth, a wailing ballad remembered by the winter hearth, the harsh exposed face of a glacier-scoured precipice, a tangled wilderness captured on canvas: all are related in a vital kinship. The wonder of that diversity and that kinship, as true of the human history as of the natural kingdom, is not diminished but increased by familiarity.

Along Canada's northeastern coast the Gaspé Peninsula curls like a frozen wave toward Newfoundland from which it is separated by the Gulf of St. Lawrence. Here begins—or ends, whichever you choose—that continental backbone of mountain ranges congregated under the single name, Appalachians. And here overlooking Percé rock is the Pic-de-l'Aurore, Peak of Dawn, where we watched the morning sun splinter its early rays on the North American continent.

Thousands of miles to the south the narrow Nantahala Gorge carves like a jagged scar through the green hills of North Carolina, its name meaning Land-of-the-Noonday-Sun a bequest from the Cherokee Indians who believed that the sun's rays could penetrate this deep canyon only at mid-day. Contrast between the Gaspé and Nantahala stabs home the prodigal variety that is part of the vitality, splendor, and tragedy of the Appalachian Mountains.

Slanting roughly northeast to southwest the Appalachians seem to be familiar to everyone and precisely known by no one. There is, for instance, no agreement regarding their length. Equally qualified authorities assert that they extend 1200 miles, 1500, and 3000 miles. There is confusion about their constituent ranges. Exactly what is included in the Longfellow Mountains? Or the Taconics? Where does the Blue Ridge or the Allegheny Range begin and end? There are numerous contradictions between popular understanding and scientific identification.

Recognizing much that is still open to controversy and speculation, let us try to orient ourselves in this complex, enticing landscape of the Appalachian Mountains.

The Appalachians can be divided into three general regions: northern, central, and southern. The northern area begins with the Long Range in the chill harshness of Newfoundland. It continues down the Notre Dame and the Shickshock ranges in Quebec and the Cape Breton Highlands of Nova Scotia to the scattered group of Longfellow Mountains in central and western Maine, the White Mountains of New Hampshire, and Vermont's Green Mountains, which become the steep Hoosacs and the amenable Berkshires in Massachusetts, Connecticut, and eastern New York. There are also the Taconics in Vermont, Massachusetts, and a sliver of New York.

The Shickshocks of this northern Appalachia, with their stunted fir and spruce forest and bleak zones of permafrost, take their odd name from Micmac Indian words meaning "rocky mountains." There are other arresting mountain names: Saddleback, Jr. and Old Speck and Sunday River Whitecap Mountain. Towering over all other northern Appalachian peaks is the forbidding, fog-bound presence of Mt. Washington, 1500 feet above timber line, whose violent storms and barren rocks have claimed more lives than any other mountain in North America. New Hampshire's mighty Mt. Monadnock has given its name to the isolated mountain formation which stands alone, resistant to the erosion that has worn away its surrounding plane. Here rise, too, Mt. Katahdin, Mt. Greylock, Mt. Mansfield, the imposing summits of the Presidential Range, and rivers with strong Indian names: the Androscoggin, Kennebec, Merrimack, Winooski, and Housatonic.

This is the region of the Mohawk Trail and New Hampshire's brooding North

Country and the "notches" (they're called "gaps" in the south and "passes" out west): Crawford, Pinkham, and Franconia, most famous of all, with its cliffs, cascades, cable car and weathered granite profile of the Old Man of the Mountains, inspiration for Nathaniel Hawthorne's classic short story. Northern Appalachia is the land of broad-chested, stout-hearted Morgan horses, ski slopes and town meetings and winter carnivals and summer music festivals, and granite that is the hardest rock in the world other than diamond, sapphire, and ruby. Robert Frost brought the bite of hard cider and harsh winters into his poems born of northern Appalachian farming.

Central Appalachia includes New York's Catskills and the beginnings of two long ranges: the Blue Ridge in southern Pennsylvania and the Alleghenies which rise in southwestern New York, reach across parts of western Pennsylvania, western Maryland, and an eastern corner of Ohio before merging into the southern region.

Sandwiched between the two rugged extremities of the Appalachian system, the central region is more subdued, more accessible to human contact. Here are the New York Highlands along the mighty Hudson (with the Storm King Highway once as breathtaking as a roller coaster to a child visitor); the Helderbergs and the stunted New Jersey Highlands; Maryland's South Mountains and Big Savage Gorge; Shickshinny and Blue and Cheat and Spruce Mountains and the Poconos. In central Appalachia the Delaware Water Gap, carved through the Kittatinny Mountains millions of years ago, provides one of the important and picturesque passages through the Appalachian barrier. Lordly rivers shape this region: the Hudson, Delaware, Mohawk, Susquehanna, Potomac, Monongahela.

This central Appalachia is the land of Dutch patroons, yesterday's famous Catskill Mountain House and today's "Borsch Belt" of mammoth hotel resorts, the tragic Johnstown flood, Hawk Mountain's annual spectacle of birds in migration; and land, too, of the Long Rifle—perfected in Pennsylvania but famous as the Kentucky Rifle, the weapon that provided distance and accuracy for frontiersmen in and beyond the Appalachian ranges. In this region coal and iron joined to create industrial empires for modern America.

In the third or southern region of the Appalachian system are the Alleghenies of West Virginia and Virginia; the Blue Ridge range extending across Virginia and western North Carolina into the northwestern corner of South Carolina and northern Georgia; the Unakas in southwestern Virginia, eastern Tennessee, and western North Carolina (of which the Great Smoky Mountains are a part); and the Cumberland Mountains of eastern Kentucky, southwestern West Virginia, eastern Tennessee and northern Alabama.

This southern region is the one most frequently associated with the word Appalachia. It is the most difficult area of the Appalachian system to identify precisely and describe clearly because it is a chaos of complex ranges, valleys, escarpments, and cross ridges that follow no orderly pattern or direction. Here the diversity of the Appalachians reaches its zenith. In his long walk across America in 1867, naturalist John Muir paused in Kentucky and called this "the most favored province of bird and flower." In addition to the major mountains already mentioned there are the majestic Blacks (lofty Mt. Mitchell is one of these cross ridges), the Craggies, the Iron Mountains and the Chilhowees, Mt. Rogers and Walden Ridge, Rock Face and Springer and Pine Mountain in Georgia, Little and Sand and Choccolocco in Alabama, and the peaks christened Bullhead, Fodderstack, Grandfather, Chunky Gal. This is the area of Virginia's Skyline Drive and North Carolina's Blue Ridge Parkway, a highland thoroughfare for noncommercial travelers who wish to take time rather than make time.

Southern Appalachia is the country of dulcimers (stringed instruments) and coal, underground caves and unexplained prehistoric stone forts, southern skiing and whitewater canoeing and peculiar mountaintop "balds" whose open grassy spaces remain scientific mysteries. It is the region of Big Bone Lick where giant mastodons died beside ancient salt springs; and Copperhill where industrial sulphur fumes burned away the earth's plant cover and left a corner of Tennessee naked and eroded as the surface of the moon; and Cumberland Gap where Americans poured westward in the wake of Daniel Boone. Among its rivers are the James, the Shenandoah, the Clinch and Holston and French Broad, the Tennessee, the Gauley and the New which form the Kanawha, the Cumberland, the Guyandotte, Cheat, Big Sandy and Kentucky, the Tallulah, the Chattooga, Chattacoochee and the Coosa.

These are the bare bold outlines of the Appalachian Mountains. Generations of explorers and settlers, artists and scientists have struggled to interpret their many facets. Writers have set their stories in the three different regions and revealed distinctive responses to many kinds of wilderness. Thirst for adventure won generations of readers for James Fenimore Cooper's frontier tale, *The Deerslayer*, in the New England woods. Cinema devotees flocked to the post-Vietnam *The Deerhunter*, rooted in Pennsylvania's snow-flecked Alleghenies. There were many who found both adventure and allegory in James Dickey's retarded villains and white-water challenges of *Deliverance* in the Georgia Blue Ridge.

There is another distinctive feature of the Appalachian system and that is its Great Valley, binding Canada to Alabama in a fertile trough furrowed between the frozen waves of successive mountain ranges. Beginning as the St. Lawrence Valley it continues as the Hudson, the Kittatinny, the Lehigh and Lebanon, the Cumberland, the Shenandoah and Valley of Virginia, and finally the Tennessee Valley and Coosa Valley. This Great Valley has provided the stage for decisive roles in American history: as the disputed frontier of contending empires; a funnel for speculators reaching westward in search of fortunes and settlers in search of homes; a battleground for brothers locked in the bloodletting of civil war; a site of bold experiment in resource control and growth.

Down the central and southern portions of the Great Valley flowed the tides of Palatine Germans (known as Pennsylvania Dutch), English, and Scotch-Irish who were to stamp their character on much of Appalachia. Mines and industries drew other national groups to settle in the mountain regions but the Scotch-Irish became the Appalachian mountaineers par excellence. They had searched for this homeland a long time. Transplanted from

Scotland to northern Ireland during the reign of James I, their efforts in farming and the woolen trade proved so successful that the English, fearing such competition, curtailed their markets and for good measure set curbs on their religious zeal as well. The result was wholesale exodus to America. Hardy, persevering, by turns dour and humorous, the Scotch-Irish character set its seal on the Appalachian highlands and valleys.

The Appalachian Mountains and hollows and coves have nurtured some of our oldest legends and sturdiest heroes. Among the Catskills rumpled old Rip Van Winkle fled his scolding wife, heard the rumble of giant bowling balls in the hills, and was startled by the world's changes when he came down from the mountains after a 20-year snooze. Through the Unakas and the Cumberlands the coonskin-capped frontiersman Davy Crockett hunted bear in the canebrakes and spun tall tales of being half horse, half alligator. His humor was boisterous, sometimes preposterous, but his *Narrative of the Life of David Crockett* was one of America's earliest autobiographies. His frontier exploits are legendary; lesser known is his defense in Congress of the rights of Cherokees to their homeland and small landholders to their claims. When his championship of these two minorities helped defeat him in his next Congressional race Crockett declared, "The voters can go to hell. I'm going to Texas." And so he did—to Texas and the Alamo and the immortality of America's "one great epic figure," according to critic Irwin Shapiro. And in the northern Alleghenies a Seneca chieftain, Handsome Lake, seized by visions and celestial messages through which his people could abandon the white renegade's whiskey and the Indian shaman's witchcraft, renewed the cultural roots of his people into the code of a religion that survives today in Iroquois Long Houses as the Old Way of Handsome Lake.

Appalachian valleys have rung with the Puritan's warning of Cotton Mather: "Go tell mankind that there are devils and witches," and the fundamentalist's shout: "Repent!" Appalachian hills have resounded with the shouts of Pennsylvania's "Paxtang Boys" wreaking vengeance for massacre in Wyoming Valley, and with the gunshots of feuding Hatfields and McCoys, the pitiful cries of Floyd Collins trapped in a dank Kentucky cave, and the lament of Aunt Molly Jackson as she marched into the coal mines singing her Depression testimonial, "Hungry Blues."

From Canada to Alabama the Appalachians have stored opulent resources: iron and coal, granite and marble, salt and oil and natural gas, copper, gold, and a wide array of lesser minerals, precious and semi-precious stones and useful clays. Feeding industries as varied as the quarries of Barre, Vermont, and the sprawling chemical complex of Charleston, West Virginia, these assets were created when the mountains themselves were being born.

Delving into the mysteries of the Appalachians' birth, whether an explanation is sought in imagination or science, requires adjustment in our perception of time. The stop-watch and calendar are not appropriate to measurements that sweep through millions of years back to a murky dawn.

Indians in the Appalachians shaped myth to resolve the riddle of creation. To the Cherokees the earth was seen as a huge island floating in a sea, suspended at the four cardinal points by a cord hung from the sky vault. The animals who lived beyond the sky sent the Great Buzzard down to make the earth ready for them. He flew low over all the ground while it was still soft. He grew tired and his wings began to flap and he dipped down to touch the ground. Wherever they struck the earth there was a valley and where the wings turned upward again there arose a mountain. When the animals above saw what was happening they became afraid that all the world would be mountains. They called the Great Buzzard back —but the Cherokee country remains full of mountains to this day.

Results of geologists' efforts to determine the origins of the Appalachian Mountains are almost as dramatic as the myth of the Great Buzzard, and as difficult to decipher. Explanations that were accepted for many years have been altered in recent years by a theory called plate tectonics. Discussing this violent drama we must compress eons of time into a few minutes, distill hundreds of centuries of alternating upheaval and dormancy into a paragraph.

Imagine first the sounds—the rum-blings and crashes and collisions—as this creation unfolded. Imagine the smells of smoke and ash, of seas serene and stagnant and rivers fresh as dawn. Imagine the thunder of continents in motion, oceans a-borning, rock driving into rock, ice grinding down pinnacles, rivers gouging out valleys. And to link this exercise in imagination to the daily present—evaluate the vast beds of coal, oil, and gas left under the Appalachian earth as largesse from the Paleozoic era; listen to the incessant clamor of gannets gathered at their nesting haunts on Canada's Bonaventure Island and consider that they are descendants of marine birds that mated on Mesozoic promontories. Look upon a modern monument or museum fashioned from Vermont granite or Tennessee marble and know that this was bonded in the dim dawn of Precambrian time. Dip into Walden Pond with awareness that it is

Rhododendron blossoms fully opened in early spring bare spectacular beauty of this native plant in southern Appalachians.

there because of the long melting of a random shard torn from retreating glaciers. In the Appalachian Mountains the past is all around us, ever present.

The Appalachians are among the oldest mountains on earth. Today they reach lesser heights than the younger Rocky Mountains because the aging process has diminished them; much of their story remains to be deciphered. The first upheaval to create sediment that would become part of the Appalachians occurred some 1100 million years ago (give or take a month) during the so-called Grenville episode of geologic time. Long ages of sedimentation alternated with periods of violent eruptions during which rocks were formed and then subjected to such extremes of heat and pressure that they were transformed into sequences of metamorphic rock. Limestone changed into marble, shale became slate and schist, sandstones were transformed into quartzite, and intrusions of magma formed bodies of granite. These rocks antedated most plant or animal life; intense pressures and heat destroyed any traces of primitive life—so that the pre-Cambrian crystalline rocks contain no trace of fossils. They form what is known as "Old" Appalachia in Canada, New England, and a belt east of the Great Valley with the Blue Ridge at its heart.

"New" Appalachia stretches to the west, made up of shales, sandstones, and coals that were created by sediments deposited, stratified, and solidified over a long span

Horses are a source of power for many maple sugaring operations. This team is gathering sap near Montpelier, Vermont.

of geological time. During the Carboniferous Period of the Paleozoic era, a warm humid interlude spawned the growth of luxuriant forests of ferns and conifers. Giant reptiles roamed steamy swamps. Then a tremendous mountain folding occurred, the Appalachian Revolution, near the end of the Paleozoic era. Interior crumpling of the earth resulted from stress placed on masses of subterranean rock. As parts of the earth buckled into folds, cracked and faulted, other parts were thrust up and these uplifts served to drive one rock mass atop another. Thus the ancient crystallines were lifted in some places above more recent sedimentary rock deposits. Subsequent carving of ice and water has continued through millions of years of building, eroding, uplifting and shaping of the Appalachians.

This long accepted answer of mountains born of inland seas and the Appalachian Revolution has itself been revolutionized by the modern hypothesis of plate tectonics, or the theory of continental drift. Science writer Walter Sullivan has defined this as "the view of our planet as everliving, ever in flux, its continents in motion with respect to one another, carried by the creeping movements of gigantic plates of the earth's crust, clashing with one another from time to time to produce the great mountain ranges."

Orchestration for this immense choreography of the continents began in that distant Grenville episode of a billion years ago. Remains of sediment accumulated from eroded Grenville summits is found today in the upthrust Great Smoky Mountains. Following this long pre-Cambrian era, there came a stately procession of episodes each lasting 100 million years or so, during which major Appalachian mountain building began, layers of granite were formed, and—most important—the Paleozoic Ocean slowly expanded. During the following Taconic episode, perhaps 450 million years ago, the ancient ocean began to shrink and as its crust slipped under the American continent, island arcs were formed and driven against the coast. During the Acadian period, 380 million years ago the European continent collided with the northern part of the North American continent, affecting the Appalachians in what is now their New England region. Culmination of this process occurred with the final contraction of the ancient Atlantic Ocean during which the continental bulge of West Africa drove against the American plate. That impact thrust up mountains higher than the present Alps in Europe, ancestors of today's Alleghenies and the southern ridge-and-valley provinces of the Appalachians including the majestic Blue Ridge. Eventually, beginning about 180 million years ago, the new Atlantic Ocean formed as the African and North American continents began to pull apart once more. Further uplifts and crumplings and major shaping by erosion pummeled the Appalachians through succeeding epochs.

Other agents besides internal revolution and/or continental drift and collision helped hew out the sharp pinnacles and scoop out the valleys and ravines in the

State capitol at Harrisburg, Pennsylvania is uniquely situated near geographical midpoint of the Appalachian Mountain Range.

Appalachians. These master carvers were water and ice.

Many of the major Appalachian rivers are older than the mountains. One of these, paradoxically named the New, is the oldest river in North America and one of the oldest in the world. During the hundred million years of mountain building and erosion that we have examined, the New was born in the collision of the African and North American continents. It flowed north and west from an eastward extension of the present Blue Ridge into a vast interior sea. Today it still flows from the Blue Ridge north and west, becomes the Kanawha in West Virginia, and empties into the Ohio. It is the only river system that cuts across the entire Appalachian plateau from east to west.

The rivers northeast of the New in Virginia flow into the Atlantic Ocean, often through dramatic passages called water gaps. Southwest of the New most of the major rivers rush toward the Ohio. When the mountains were raised up, blocking rivers' westward course to the shallow sea or trough that once covered mid-America, these old rivers sought out their own routes, creating spectacular gorges, canyons, and "narrows" that are now a superlative part of Appalachian scenery. In their thrust toward the Mississippi some of these rivers have been called cantakerous, not unlike the people who would one day live along many of them. Some larger streams to the south, dominated by the sinuous meandering of the Tennessee, follow that river's example, trying several courses before arriving at the Ohio. Exceptions are those rivers rising southeastward on the Blue Ridge, which flow into the Atlantic, and Chattahoochee, running from the northeastern corner of Georgia and southwestward into the Gulf of Mexico.

Insistent waters have contoured the land of the Appalachians. But only one area of the Appalachian Mountains endured the ponderous assaults of glaciers and, as poet Robert Frost said of diverging roads in one of his New England poems, "that has made all the difference."

Colossal ice sheets pressed south from Labrador several times during the Pleistocene Age. In wave after wave they covered the Appalachians of Canada, New England, New York, New Jersey, northern Pennsylvania and Ohio. Only 20,000 years ago the ice cover over these northern and central Appalachians reached its maximum, and began a slow retreat that continued during the next five to ten thousand years.

As the huge thaw set in, melting bodies of ice that stood a mile and more thick, massive slides of topsoil and gravel tobogganed across the land. Boulders sheared off pinnacles and slopes, exposed granite was scraped smooth and bare. Drift, made up of clay, stone, and sand, piled up across valleys, creating sites for future lakes. Maverick chunks of ice hurtled into the earth and as they melted gradually formed "kettles" which would become New England's famous ponds. Mt. Katahdin, one of the best known mountain masses of the Appalachian system, rises today above the forests of central Maine like a splendid sculpture from the Ice Age. The northeast wall of Baxter Peak, its towering summit, is the highest rock face in the U.S. Appalachians. Its narrow serrated Knife Edge Ridge, its basins and boulders and moraine belts, represent dramatic debris accumulated in one of nature's ancient workshops. Little wonder that the Indians

believed this mountain to be the council place of the gods and called it Kette-Adene, the "Great Mountain."

Much of the striking contrast between the northern and southern Appalachian Mountains arises from the fact that the long freeze alternating with the powerful tumbling and scouring of ice never reached the southern Appalachians. Lakes gouged out by glacial action are scattered by the hundreds across the northern mountains. The largest natural lake wholly within the U.S. Appalachian system is in Maine, 32-mile long Moosehead Lake from which the Kennebec River flows. The southern Appalachians are characterized by many streams. For instance, in the entire Great Smoky Mountains National Park there's no still water, not one lake or pond, but a complex network of flowing water ranging from tiny rivulets to rushing rivers.

The ice that buried the northern Appalachians drove plants and animals south for survival. These migrants found refuge in the high hills and valleys of the southern Appalachians. Thus caribou once foraged in Tennessee and the wooly mammoth plodded across parts of Pennsylvania. Arctic plants took root in the compatible habitat they found in the higher elevations of the Blue Ridge, the Unakas, the Great Smokies, the Cumberlands. The southern region of Appalachia became the seedbed for its northern neighbors. Although many of the animals disappeared, became extinct, numerous plants remained in the hospitable locality. Today in the Great Smokies a rich variety of life is preserved.

Within this park are 1400 varieties of flowering plants, 30 species of salamanders (far more than in any other area in the world), more varieties of trees (about 130 species) than can be found in all of western Europe, and a habitat of northern altitudes in southern latitudes that allows many birds to stay at home here throughout the year and migrate vertically (up into the high forests during summer, down to protected valleys during the winter).

Among the unusual mementoes remaining from the Pleistocene glaciers are the bogs—often called glades by local residents and labeled Southern muskegs by more precise naturalists. Most of these natural refrigerators occur in the Alleghenies of Pennsylvania, Virginia, and

West Virginia. To the uninitiated Virginia's Burkes Garden or West Virginia's Cranberry Glades may appear to be only strange misplaced arctic tundra or swampy wasteland of matted vegetation and troublesome muck. To the ornithologist, botanist, biologist, or simply curious explorer, however, the insect-devouring plants, orchids, mosses, animals, and birds offer a glimpse of some of the oddities and mysteries of a web of life extending far back in time, to America's Great Ice Age.

Many of the waterfalls in the northeastern Appalachians are also creations of the ice age. Glacial moraine forced streams into new beds and over terrace-like shelves of solidified debris. The results include such fine waterfalls as those embellishing New Hampshire's Crawford Notch, and nearby Franconia, Kinsman, and Pink-

Numerous fishing villages along the shore of Gaspe Peninsula designate the northern end of the Appalachian Mountain Range.

ham Notches. In the southern Appalachians waterfalls are often the result of a contention between hard and soft rock formations thrust together during those ancient upheavals. Soft rock has been worn away under the constant flow of streams, leaving shelves and valley rims of harder, stubborn rock. (Limestone has been called "a poor fighter.") Fall Creek Falls in Tennessee is an especially dramatic example of this action, cascading 257 feet over a semi-circular cliff, its fall higher than that of Niagara. In the Allegheny front of northern Alabama the Little River carves a gorge through Lookout Mountain that may be the deepest river gorge in eastern America, creating along its course two scenic waterfalls. Providing power, especially along the fall line of the eastern

Mid-winter generosity is fully expressed in the well maintained village of Weston, nestled in the Green Mountains of Vermont.

slopes, or offering an unexpected bonus of refreshing beauty, waterfalls lace the Appalachian ranges.

Forged in a long, violent, awesome past, the Appalachian mountains and their rivers have influenced the brief course of human history on this continent. Indian nations used the fertile valleys and let the rugged ranges serve as barriers defining shifting tribal ambitions and power. European settlers remained shackled to the eastern coast for more than a century before they overcame the forbidding mountain barricade. When the thrust into and beyond the mountains began, however, it quickened to a floodtide, challenging the builders of homes and cities, stirring the imaginations of musicians and artists and tellers of tales, kindling visions of wealth that could paradoxically enrich and impoverish generations to follow.

Europeans were a long time coming to the Appalachian Mountains. After 1524, when a Florentine navigator named Verrazano, in the hire of the French king Francis I, prowled along the New England coast and sighted mountains to the west, more than a century passed before the French explorer, Samuel de Champlain, on the lake that was to bear his name, spied Mt. Mansfield and exclaimed, according to abiding legend, "Les Verts Monts!" giving the mountains their eventual English name and suggesting the French name by which a future state would be known.

It was an arrogant, battle-scarred, gold-greedy Spanish conquistador, Hernando De Soto, who plunged into the southern wilderness and became the first European

to actually explore a wide swath of the Appalachian Mountains. He rode at the head of a strange caravan. In 1539-1540 De Soto and some 600 men (many of them wearing heavy armor), more than 200 horses, a pack of fighting hounds, with captive Indian women and burden-bearers and their own commissary-on-the-hoof, a herd of squealing, foraging hogs, struggled through the Blue Ridge and Unaka ranges of South Carolina, North Carolina, and Tennessee to the Alabama hills. They continued westward to the banks of the Mississippi where a disillusioned De Soto succumbed to fever and was buried in the great river.

The season was spring when De Soto's columns trudged through the southern Appalachians, a rare and pleasant time of year. The tough tenacious soldiers were looking for pearls and gold but they found, according to their journals, wild roses, lavish forests, and wild strawberries "savoury, palatable, and fragrant" growing so thick they "covered the ground as with a red cloth." Despite these bounties and those shared by their awed, ingenuous hosts along the way, the trail of pillage, fire, deception and death De Soto blazed through the Indian villages and virgin wilderness was brutally prophetic. It would be almost two centuries before that major influx of English, Germans and Scotch-Irish arrived to claim portions of the Appalachians but the Southern Indians' suspicion of the white intruders had not been erased, was, in fact, firmly entrenched.

Another significant result of that amazing journey: it was De Soto who gave these mountains their Indian name. A Muskhogean tribe living in northwest Florida was called by the Choctaws "Apalachees," meaning "people on the other side." Although these Indians had no known association with the extended mountain chain of which the Spanish expedition glimpsed only a small segment, De Soto captured something of the meaning and history of those mountains in his choice of their name.

In this early contact of white European with the red native and the green wilderness there were seeds of the human responses that would devastate or conserve, evaluate or celebrate, shape or be shaped by the natural world of the Appalachian

Mountains. One response was that of the Indian already at home in this land.

For the Indian there were bonds of kinship between himself and all that was alive in the world around him. Such a relationship meant, for instance, that the Cherokees, those mountaineers of the Southern tribes, did not use in their language male and female genders but instead used genders of animate and inanimate. Animate included plants and trees as well as animals and people. A Quaker observer understood the reason for this: "All animated nature, in whatever degree, is in their eyes a great whole from which they have not yet ventured to separate themselves."

Just such separation was the essence of the second response to the resources of the Appalachians. From De Soto on there were those who sought in these splendid mountains only an answer to their own ravenous appetite for instant wealth, personal glory, superficial pleasure, power. And with each new fragmentation that fed that appetite the "great whole" suffered.

Witness: the handsome plump-breasted passenger pigeons whose migrations through the Appalachian Mountains were so massive that forests were broken by their roosting. Audubon, great painter of birds, estimated that in a single four-day flight over Kentucky one billion passenger pigeons darkened the noonday skies. The slaughter of them was so relentless and wasteful that Theodore Roosevelt could say of their extinction: "It is possible that humanity will produce a new Rembrandt; but it is impossible to produce a new Passenger Pigeon." Its extinction, he said, came because "our people were not civilized . . . it belonged to every creature with a shot gun and no conscience."

Witness: the rare ginseng (valued so highly in the herbal medicine of China), delicate pink moccasin flower and yellow lady slipper, shortia and maidenhair fern that are only tokens of the plant life that the renowned botanist, Asa Gray, called more than a century ago "the choicest botanical treasures which the country affords;" many of them poised today on the brink of extinction, their habitat pushed deeper and deeper into the disappearing wilderness.

Witness: the dispossession of people from their homeland. There was the devastation of the proud five nations of the Iroquois: the Seneca, Cayuga, Onondaga, Oneida, and Mohawk. In battle they were said to "approach like foxes, fight like lions, and disappear like birds." There was the scattering of the five "civilized tribes" of the south: Creek, Catawba, Choctaw, Chickasaw, and Cherokee, the last of whom were driven from their highland farms when gold was discovered in a mountain creek in Georgia. Along their "trail of tears" westward a fourth of the 14,000 Cherokees on this long march died under the lash of winter sleet and snow and despair. One obstinate little band held out in the rough terrain along the North Carolina-Tennessee border where U.S. General Winfield Scott found it too costly to send his soldiers for their capture, and these Cherokees won for their descendants the Qualla Reservation still existing today, home of the eastern band of their tribe.

Bird and animal, plant and human, each is related to the whole no less than the mountains in their rocky chains are linked. To grow up in the Appalachians is to have access to this sense of kinship. The name of the stream tumbling in front of our home—and how many Beaverdam creeks and ponds and counties are there scattered throughout the Appalachian Mountains?—even that name is a connection, improbable as it may seem, to the first weak stabs toward Appalachian settlement and the ferocious French and Indian War of the mid-1700's. How so? The link is in the earliest treasure exploited throughout the Appalachians.

Those early Europeans discovered something more accessible, more plentiful than legendary gold glistening in the streams and hills. They beheld the shining pelts of beaver. Deer, elk, buffalo, otter—the skins of these, too, were valuable but it was the appetite for beaver to meet the demands of European fashion in hats and coats that seemed to be insatiable. It was the industrious beaver as much as any other single factor that propelled France and England into their contest for control of the American continent.

That war was as decisive, as vicious, as complex as any engagement America has suffered, yet it remains relatively little known. At its core was the Appalachian frontier and the rich interior country that stretched westward—a frontier where the commerce and worldwide ambitions of two empires were joined in a definitive conflict. The pawns were proud red warriors and innocent Indian villages, as well as the stubborn European settlers in lonely little forts strung thinly along the long blue wall of mountains and valleys.

At their first meeting with the New World's Indian tribes the Frenchman Samuel de Champlain and the Dutchman Henry Hudson promptly exchanged knives and hatchets and other iron tools for beaver and other skins. Fur was the magnet drawing the first trading post to the edge of Virginia's Appalachian wilderness in the mid-seventeenth century.

Abraham Wood's Fort Henry was ostensibly for the protection of white settlements against Indian attack. Actually the primary interest of Wood and his sponsor, Virginia Governor William Berkeley, was the rich Indian fur trade. Northward, a trading post where Mohawk and Hudson rivers joined was named Beverwyck in recognition of its chief commodity. When New York moved from Dutch to British control Beverwyck became Albany.

While the European craving for beaver seemed to be boundless the Indian's reliance on iron goods grew more entrenched. Once upon a time he had hunted and trapped to fulfill his own needs of food and clothing. Now he hunted to supply goods for a market. There seemed no limit to the boatloads of furs that floated down the rivers or swayed in cumbersome bundles lashed to the backs of long trains of packhorses winding through the wilderness. As early as 1640 the Mohawk and Hudson river valleys were already stripped of their beaver. There was continuous pressure to quest for new sources.

It was a bloody business, the skin trade. It led to bloody wars. Wars among Indian tribes were no longer those of ritual vengeance or tribal rivalry limited to a certain range. Now the Appalachian frontier from Canada to the Tennessee country blazed with skirmishes and battles to determine who would dominate the lucrative sources of fur—and who would receive the rewards in European goods, especially guns. The red natives' relations to each other and to the wilderness they inhabited was forever altered, tilted to a new balance— or imbalance—where tribes could be extinguished, where a species of animal or plant could be decimated.

For almost a century English and French contest for power in other parts of the world kindled a series of struggles in America, the dirty little wars so royally named for King William, Queen Anne, King George. During these combats there were numerous different alignments among Europeans and Indians, each leaving in its wake a bitter residue of hate and suspicion as each war dragged to an inconclusive finish.

In 1754 the rivalry of a century and longer reached across the ocean once more and embroiled struggling American colonists and Indians in a final convulsion. A prize of that contest would be the harvest of furs flowing from America's rivers and forests. Their response to these rich natural resources of the New World represented the two routes by which France and England sought conquest and possession of this land. England followed the way of settlement, moving inland from the Atlantic Ocean to the great Appalachian barrier. France was committed to trade, reaching down from the St. Lawrence along the Mississippi River, probing its Appalachian tributaries, in search of furs. French plans to encircle the English and keep them pinned to the seaboard east of the mountains met ready resistance from Englishmen who were no less (but less exclusively) interested in trade.

When Virginia's Governor Alexander Spotswood attired in plumed hat and green velvet led the first expedition across the summit of the Blue Ridge in 1716, he toasted his companions in numerous rounds of wine and celebration. (Later he would present each member of his sprightly party with a jewel-studded golden horseshoe, a memento of their journey over the mountains' rough terrain, initiating them as the Knights of the Golden Horseshoe.) Beneath the merrymaking and the pageantry, however, there was a serious purpose prompting this veteran who had fought the French at Blenheim. Spotswood welcomed the fact that "Nature formed a Barrier for us by that long Chain of Mountains which run from the back of South Carolina as far as New York, and which are only passable some few places." The English were resolute in their determination to promote both settlement and trade warned about the possibility of the French "engrossing the whole Skin Trade." And into and beyond the mountains. They wanted neither competitors nor enemies in the back country.

Forced to choose in this ancient tug-of-war between France and England, powerful Indian tribes perceived that their survival would be more likely alongside the temporary presence of French trading posts than disputing over the establishment of permanent English homesites. They took up the tomahawk and the rifle on the side of the French.

The Indians had long since become acquainted with the fierceness of English determination to make homes on Indian lands. An effort in 1675 to dislodge a wedge of settlers had resulted in the bloodiest battle ever fought on New England soil. Involving 1,000 Massachusetts and Connecticut militiamen and 3,000 Narragansetts, the conflict lasted a mere three hours but left two-thirds of the Indians slaughtered or burned to death in their village, with a loss of 80 colonists. Similar bloody engagements had dotted the length of the eastern seaboard as settlers ebbed inland to the mountains. Now, taking advantage of the French and English rivalry, Indian leaders hoped to turn back decisively the settlers' ever-widening grasp —and at the same time increase their own hold on the fur trade.

The French and Indian War began in the Appalachian Mountains in 1754 when a 21-year-old major in the Virginia militia

Daisies bobbing in summer breeze render change of pace after discovery in secluded area on Gaspe Peninsula of Quebec.

named George Washington was sent by Virginia Governor Dinwiddie to inform a party of French soldiers probing along the headwaters of the Allegheny and to the Forks of the Ohio that they were on Virginia's soil. Since Washington and Dinwiddie were both members of a group called the Ohio Company, formed to promote fur trading and western settlement, a company whose generous half-million acre grant lay west of the mountains, there were colonists who felt that Washington's and Dinwiddie's interest in the French presence was sparked by private as well as public concern. These colonists paid reluctant heed to their leaders' call to arms.

The French and Indian War ended in 1763 with English conquest of Canada and France's cession of her American empire. During those nine years of war death and destruction ravaged the Appalachian Mountain settlements. At an aptly named little defense post, Fort Necessity, near present Uniontown, Pennsylvania, George Washington met an early defeat.

A greater defeat followed. Reports that the French planned to establish their defense perimeter along the crests of the Alleghenies rather than along the Ohio River led to the Crown's commitment to full-scale war in the colonies. Sir Edward Braddock and British forces were sent to destroy the French threat. 1400 Redcoats, 450 Virginia militia, attendant bagpipers, scouts, and slaves toiled over roadless mountains and through the gaps only to be ambushed near their destination of Fort Duquesne, with Braddock killed and his army decimated.

The back country of New England, New York, Pennsylvania, Virginia and the Carolinas was now subjected to the fierce border warfare that those settlers and their descendants never forgot. Massacres and kidnappings and torture were not confined to soldiers or warriors but became a part of family experience and memory. From the Susquehanna Valley an Indian trader's report of settlers' flights described the situation in other valleys too at the height of the terror. "The roads are full of starved, naked, indigent multitudes," he said. Along the Shenandoah valley "the smoke of burning plantations darkens the day and hides the neighboring mountains from our sight."

The disastrous situation began to change only after another British foray— this time with an army 6,000 strong cutting its own road across the mountains— brought about the destruction of Fort Duquesne and French retreat from the site which saw the prompt construction of Fort Pitt, whose name would be incorporated into that of the city to rise at the crucial Forks of the Ohio. With the fall of Quebec in 1759 British dominion over North America was assured. Settlers and speculators could look once again to the Appalachians and beyond.

At the close of the French and Indian War the Appalachians were assigned another role in history. The British government was troubled by the breakdown in relations with the Indian tribes and the threat that had been mobilized by a powerful chief named Pontiac. Significant overtures of friendship were extended to the tribes. Most important of these was a concession proclaiming that the lands beyond the Appalachian Mountains belonged to the Indians. In fact, land lying within some of the Appalachian ranges was included in the Indian territory set aside by this line of demarcation. White settlers were denied access to this territory. Thus it was hoped earlier tensions could be soothed and trade with Indians restored.

Of course, it did not work out that way. The frontier people had no more intention of honoring the legal barrier posed by the king's line down the Appalachians than they had of being put off by the harsh physical barrier the mountains presented. George Washington had penetrated this Appalachian country; he also understood his king's forked tongue. Communicating with a soldier who had served in his regiment he voiced the common perception shared by his countrymen when he wrote in confidence that he could never look upon the proclamation of 1763 as other than "a temporary expedient to quiet the minds of the Indians."

Such expedients had long since become familiar to the Indians and this one quieted neither their minds nor those of land-hungry speculators and settlers. Dissatisfaction with this demarcation line became one of the grievances separating the Crown and the colonies.

When the last bonds uniting Great

Britain and the American colonies were finally broken the Revolutionary War in the Appalachian country assumed many aspects of the French and Indian War. North and south the Indian tribes allied themselves with the British. Appalachia's Mohawk and Cherry valleys in New York, Wyoming Valley in Pennsylvania, the Holston and Watauga and Nolichucky settlements on Virginia's and North Carolina's western borders, and many other outposts down the length of the Appalachians were exposed to guerilla attack and massacre. Settlements in Virginia's back country and the "dark and bloody ground" known as Kaintuck suffered such devastation during 1777 that the year was afterward remembered as "the year of the terrible sevens."

Loyalties divided between Patriots and Loyalists were as bitter in the Appalachian country as elsewhere across the suffering land. When Lord Cornwallis was sent south in a British strategy to win final and decisive victory in that theater of war, Patriot hopes were at their lowest ebb as he launched a three-pronged march from Charleston northward. Then his most brilliant officer, Major Patrick Ferguson, made a crucial mistake. He sent word to the Appalachian frontiersmen that if they did not join the king's cause British forces would march over the mountains, hang their leaders and lay their country waste with fire and sword. No ultimatum could have been better designed to unify and arouse mountain people. Riding their own horses, carrying pouches of food they had provided themselves, wearing their practical buckskin shirts and white-brimmed hats and homespun breeches, clutching their prized long rifles, a volunteer army swept down from the Unakas and the Blue Ridge in October, 1780, and demolished Patrick Ferguson's army on a South Carolina summit named Kings Mountain. It was a turning point in the southern campaign. Their mission accomplished, the mountaineers returned to their homes to ward off possible Indian attacks. Cornwallis, stunned by the proportions of the defeat at Kings Mountain, was delayed in his sweep up the coast—which led finally to Yorktown.

A kindred spirit of individualism and independence radiated from Ethan and Ira Allen and their Green Mountain Boys in their determination to establish the state of Vermont before, during and after the Revolution. Ethan Allen was the hero of Ticonderoga's early capture from the British and he did not intend for the American Continental Congress to "capture" Vermont by following a proposal to cut it in half along the ridge of the Green Mountains, thus giving one half to New Hampshire and the other half to New York. At one point he thundered, "I am as resolutely determined to defend the independence of Vermont as Congress is that of the United States, and rather than fail will retire with hardy Green Mountain Boys into the desolate Caverns and Mountains, and wage war with human nature at large." Appalachian mountaineers are not easily discouraged.

With the close of the Revolutionary War Americans were ready to discover Appalachia's treasure. One of those treasures was the great Appalachian forest. Stretching from Canada to Alabama it was one of the wonders of the continent.

Two distinctive features of this forest were its deciduous hardwoods and its white pines. Today the best and most extensive broadleaved deciduous forests in the world remain in the Appalachian Mountains and bordering areas, especially in southern Appalachia. Each autumn pilgrimages from across the country still pay homage to their brilliant foliage flaunting luminous hickory gold and maple scarlet and wine-red oak across the landscape. The northern hardwoods of this deciduous forest include sugar maple, red and white oak, beech, ash, birch, and buckeye. Farther south large stands of hickory, poplar, walnut, and sycamore are added. Dogwood is "the spring snow" lighting up Appalachia's hills and valleys. Another factor of this deciduous forest is its lavish ground cover of wildflowers. In early spring the trees are still stripped of their leaves and this allows sunlight to penetrate even the heavy woods. The light encourages a wealth of delicate blossoms—the trilliums and phloxes and violets among others.

Each of these hardwoods and the complex plant life nourished by their forest made a significant contribution to the household economy of the Appalachian people. Their use ranged from logs and roof shingles and floor puncheons for building a home to medicines for curing a dozen ailments. As giant lumber companies discovered these hardwood forests in Appalachia's first surge of industry, their methods and profits portended the extractive nature of much of the mountains' economy in generations to come.

The other feature unique to the virgin Appalachian forest was a belt of magnificent white pines stretching from Canada to southwest Pennsylvania. The white pine was one of the earliest victims of Europeans' awe and destruction.

Initially the stands of pine seemed overwhelming. Their dark evergreen boughs swept like waves toward the horizon. Not everyone found this a glorious prospect. In fact, the forest blanketing much of the Appalachian region seemed strange and oppressive to people who had come from countries long since denuded of wilderness. Under the closed crown of tall pines the sunlight filtered dimly, creating a twilight world that was gloomy and alien. Sounds of wind soughing through the pines deepened the sense of loneliness.

An English visitor found fault with the trees that blotted out panoramic vistas: "There is too much wood; and, when on the barren peak of some rocky hill, you catch a distant view, it generally is nothing but an undulating surface of impenetrable forest." To others the silence of the big woods was formidable.

Both the dusky gloom and the quiet were soon broken by the sharp axes of the lumberjacks. Maine is an especially appropriate place to consider the tall pines and their fate. From the Maine woods we have two testimonials that represent opposed viewpoints and responses stirred by many facets of the Appalachian Mountains' resources and history. Thus, John Springer and Henry Thoreau represented generations of discord and conflict as they reacted to the majesty of Maine's white pines.

Maine has been called "the birthplace of grandscale American logging." Its forests provided naval stores for England, especially tall masts to grace their fleet of ships. The abundance, size and versatility of the white pines made them the logger's prize. Their supply seemed boundless; they could always grow back. Vigor, ingenuity and raw physical satisfaction of felling the Maine woods was captured in the unusual memoir-treatise of a native lumberjack, John S. Springer. Through the mid-19th century Springer worked "among the wild mountains, forests, lakes and rivers of Maine," and his book bore a title as expansive as his knowledge: *Forest Life and Forest Trees, Comprising Winter Camp Life Among the Loggers and Wildwood Adventure, with Descriptions of Lumbering Operations on the Various Rivers of Maine and New Brunswick.*

State capitol at Montpelier, Vermont accepts full thrust of winter in the Green Mountains. This gold-domed granite building was designed by George Perkins Marsh, who was likely America's first ecologist.

"I was reared among the noble pines of Maine," Springer wrote, acknowledging the awe he sensed as he listened to the wind in their boughs and gazed at their massive trunks. The moment he described in most vivid detail, however, was that in which he brought down the tallest giant of them all, 144 feet tall. "I was employed about one hour and a quarter in felling it," he remembered. "After chopping an hour or so, the mighty giant, the growth of centuries, which had withstood the hurricanes and raised itself in peerless majesty above all around, began to tremble under the strokes of a mere insect, as I might appear in comparison with it. My heart palpitated as I occasionally raised my eye to its pinnacle to catch the first indication of its fall. It came down at length with a crash which seemed to shake 100 acres, while the loud echo rang through the forest, dying away among the distant hills...the surface of the stump was sufficiently capacious to allow a yoke of oxen to stand upon it ... The butt log was so large that the stream did not float it in the spring, when the drive was taken down, we were obliged to leave it behind, much to our regret and loss."

More than anger surfaced, answering another scribe of the Maine woods. Henry David Thoreau read Springer's account of prowess with the axe and proclaimed that the noble pines of Maine had not grown "to become the footstool of oxen." He growled, "Why, my dear sir, the tree might have stood on its own stump, and a great deal more comfortably and firmly than a yoke of oxen can, if you had not cut it down. What right have you to celebrate the virtues of the man you murdered?"

Their difference was more than a "feud between the poets and the choppers." In Springer and Thoreau were joined those opposing attitudes toward the natural world which have affected all of Appalachian history. Thoreau would write of his stay in the Maine woods: "The mission of men there seems to be, like so many busy demons, to drive the forest all out of the country, from every solitary beaver swamp and mountainside as soon as possible." (He might have grimaced at the boast more than a century later that Maine mills "turn out 26,000,000,000 toothpicks annually.")

Certainly Thoreau would have bristled at a report issued by the U.S. Secretary of Agriculture just after the turn of the century. It dealt with forests to the south but it echoed familiar concerns: "Standing on any of these elevated mountains (of the Blue Ridge and the Unakas and their complex network of cross ridges), one may see stretching out in either of several directions an endless succession of mountain ridges and mountain peaks . . . In every direction the splendid hard-wood forests cover and protect the mountain slopes and the countless springs of water which flow from them as the sources of great rivers. There is but one discordant fact—the calamitous destruction of the forests on these mountain slopes."

This destruction was due to the carelessness of small farmers who cultivated slopes too steep to hold top-soil once it was disturbed and, in larger measure, to the lumbermen whose reach grew incessantly longer as the railroads penetrated remote mountain valleys. "In these operations," the report charged, "there has naturally been no thought for the future. (Naturally?) Trees have been cut so as to fall along the line of least resistance regardless of what they crush. Their tops and

branches, instead of being piled in such way and burned at such time as would do the least harm, are left scattered among the adjacent growth to burn when driest, and thus destroy or injure everything within reach. The home and permanent interests of the lumberman are generally in another state or region, and his interest in these mountains begins and ends with the hope of profit."

No voice as eloquent as Thoreau's challenged the ravaging of the southern Appalachian forest but there were two developments that reflected the naturalist's long range anxieties. One was beginning of the first school of forestry in the United States and the other was founding of the Great Smoky Mountains National Park.

In 1895 construction of George Vanderbilt's Biltmore House was completed. The mansion, patterned after a chateaux in France's Loire Valley, sat on an estate of some 100,000 acres near Asheville, North Carolina. To this vast wooded tract Vanderbilt, who had seen and admired the Black Forest of Germany, brought forester and conservationist Gifford Pinchot and when Pinchot moved on to the national scene he left a sturdy Prussian, Dr. Carl Schenck, to tend the Biltmore domain and develop constructive forestry practices. On Vanderbilt's estate Schenck found it necessary to handle hardwoods he had never known in Europe, operate a band sawmill such as he had never seen used before, and work with mountain people who were proudly individualistic and totally untutored in forest conservation. He was not a patient man—the little Tyrolean hat he wore was handy in moments of frustration when he could tear it from his head and stomp on it. Schenck was not a diplomat; his local nickname was "the Kaiser." But he was determined to meet the challenge of wedding conservation to commerce in the Appalachian forest. In 1898, in a beautiful sanctuary called the Pink Beds because of the surrounding profusion of blooming rhododendron and laurel, he initiated the first classes in the United States in forest practice. Their work achieved wide renown and was firmly established by the time Schenck was required to return to Germany at the beginning of World War I. Before he departed the imperious old master stood amidst a grove of tall yellow poplars and told "his boys" of that first forestry school good-bye. "That isn't a stand of poplar," he confided. "That's a dream of my life."

The Great Smoky Mountains National Park was also the result of a dream, first orated nationally and most eloquently by a retired St. Louis librarian turned mountaineer-naturalist-sociologist: Horace Kephart. There is a certain irony in the fact that this ultimate loner should be the agent for creating in his cherished wilderness the national park that would be most heavily visited in the whole national park system.

At age 42 Kephart left his academic profession and his family and dove into that "mysterious realm" he called the "housetop of eastern America." He spent the rest of his life in the Great Smokies becoming intimately acquainted with the woods and with his mountain neighbors. He studied their history, observed their habits, participated in their daily rounds of living in an isolated, often hostile, natural setting. The book, *Our Southern Highlanders*, drawn from his observations and experiences, became a classic. What he sought in coming to these mountains was what later generations of visitors, thronging by the millions, would also seek. "In Far Appalachia," Kephart declared, "it seemed that I might realize the past in the present, seeing with my own eyes what life must have been to my pioneer ancestors of a century or two ago. Besides, I wanted to enjoy a free life in the open air, the thrill of exploring new ground, the joys of the chase, and the man's game of matching my woodcraft against the forces of nature, with no help from servants or hired guides."

Flowing like a green mantle along the dividing line between Tennessee and North Carolina, the 800 square miles of the Great Smoky Mountains National Park still shelters that "past in the present" as well as its natural variety. The pioneer experience characteristic of much of the Appalachian Mountain region has left fascinating mementoes in hidden little valleys, along bold streams, and especially in a fertile spacious expanse known as Cade's Cove. Here are cabins and frame houses, barns, smokehouses and beegums, little churches and lonely cemeteries, creaking old waterwheels — each testifying to the needs and ingenuity of the peo-

ple who once called this wilderness home.

Today this wilderness shelters the most extensive forest of virgin red spruce and unspoiled hardwoods to be found in the United States. Considering that before the park arrived an estimated two billion feet of lumber had been removed from the area, not to mention "timber shipped in the log, that which was cut only for tanbark in the early days, that cut in the woods but never brought to the mill, that destroyed in operations by machinery and fire, or that used for construction and fuel," considering this it may seem a wonder that even nature's survival and renewal powers made any park possible. One asset contributing to the survival of the red spruce was the height and inaccessibility of many Great Smokies' peaks. For 36 continuous miles these mountains maintain an altitude of more than 5000 feet. Sixteen of the pinnacles rise more than 6000 feet.

These altitudes make possible the survival of plant and animal species that were pushed south in the ancient Ice Age. Here they mingle with specimens at home in southern latitudes to create the complex system of southern plant growth known as the "Appalachian forest." One of the great floral provinces of the earth, it supports trees that bear luxuriant bloom, among them the serviceberry (locally known as "sarvis"), redbud, hawthorne, tulip poplar, dogwood, and the sourwood that fills so many purposes: as a source of delicious honey and tough sledrunners and shiny scarlet foliage in earliest autumn. Among the profusion of flowering shrubs are several whose kin flourish in the distant Orient. Most spectacular of these are the rose and purple and creamy white rhododendron, dazzling orange and yellow azalea, and dainty mountain laurel.

Almost 350 mosses and liverworts, 230 lichens, and more than 2000 fungi add to the diversity of life in the Great Smokies. Some 200 varieties of game and songbirds use this green kingdom. Although the ponderous trail-blazing bison and lordly elk, the quick cougar and gray wolf were long since extinguished in this habitat, white-tailed deer, fox, raccoon, wild boar, and the popular black bear are among animals that now roam the Park. In the 600 miles of rushing streams, trout and other prized varieties of fresh water fish abound.

Those streams are born of the heavy rainfall in the southern Appalachians, often as high as 90 inches a year on the western slope of the Great Smokies. Destruction of forest cover in areas outside the protected park aids in quick run-off of rainfall which may come in sudden heavy downpours.

Destructive floods were once part of the history of the region. To contain these floods and harness the might of an entire river system a bold federal experiment was begun in 1933. Called the Tennessee Valley Authority, its purposes were flood control, power production, navigation, land reclamation, and watershed development. Its series of extensive reservoirs, called the "Great Lakes of the South," lie within or adjoining the Appalachians. The TVA has altered the human and natural history of the region, using Appalachian water power to produce electrical and nuclear power, enlarging industrial, agricultural, and recreational opportunities. None of the changes has been without its benefits and its penalties. One of the controversial and ironic actions of the TVA in recent years has been its use of strip-mined coal to help generate electrical power. The agency whose commission included soil improvement and awareness of environmental interdependence has contributed to the ruination of vast areas of the Appalachian Mountains through its purchases of coal wrenched from mountain slopes and crests through "efficiency" of stripping.

Coal, called by Emerson "the portable climate," was and is another treasure of the Appalachian Mountains. If there was nothing noble about the buried coal beds as there had been about the lofty pines, they were awesome in their range and size. According to the U.S. Department of the Interior the single most valuable mineral deposit in the world today is that thick seam of coal stretching across western Pennsylvania, southwestern Virginia, West Virginia, much of eastern Kentucky, eastern Tennessee, and northern Alabama.

Of the many ironies of Appalachian history none is sharper than the poverty of that very Appalachian heartland holding the region's richest resource. Beneath the surface of West Virginia alone geologists estimate that the original recoverable reserve of coal amounted to some 50 billion tons. (The figures here require that same expanded imagination that can deal with the spans of geologic time during which the immense seams of coal were laid down.) An estimated 33 billion tons still remain in Kentucky's hills and valleys. Yet parts of West Virginia and Kentucky became during the 1960's symbols of twentieth century America's pockets of poverty. Yielding to this paradox of poverty amidst plenty was the situation summarized in that government report regarding southern Appalachian timber operations: the owner "is generally in another state or region, and his interest in these mountains begins and ends with the hope of profit."

Appalachian coal has been secured at

Pemigewasset Wilderness area in New Hampshire's White Mountains is a vast drainage area for crystal clear water, reached only by a hiking trail. The young girl on chute is photographer's daughter.

an ungodly sacrifice of human life. Explosions, cave-ins, accidents, carbon monoxide gas, "fire damp". From 1910 to 1933 more than 50,000 men who went into the mines were killed. More than a million were injured. These figures do not include the men whose lungs were coated with the black dust that could choke away the breath of life.

Ballads were born of those experiences "dark as a dungeon, deep in the mine." It has been more difficult to adequately mourn the power of gargantuan bulldozers and augers at work on the hillsides. Surface mining, this stripping of the mountains is called, as the "overburden" is wrenched, uprooted, and pushed aside to reach the seams of coal near the top of the ground. Overburden is a euphemism for that complex system of trees, plants, humus, and the unseen web of life they nourish, to make its destruction seem insignificant.

These mines enrich some of America's greatest fortunes.

Kentucky lawyer-conservationist Harry Caudill has looked at the Appalachian coal beds and observed: "This may be the oldest forest of its kind on the planet. This forest was here when the Rockies rose up and when they went down and when they rose up again. It has withstood two great sieges by glaciers. But it couldn't withstand a single assault by the Mellons."

Because surface mining is carried on in precipitous terrain, it creates special problems. It has been pointed out that "there is nothing much simpler or more economical than blasting away mountain tops, breaking up the seams of exposed coal and hauling it away in trucks. Gravity, however, is definitely a problem because it brings the blasted rocks and earth and acid wastes down into the hollows where people live, uprooting their trees, burying their fields and sometimes their homes, and polluting their streams." Acid drainage has been identified as the toughest problem in America today.

Once again, our oldest frontier, the Appalachian Mountains, becomes our newest frontier. Can we unlock its opulent store of energy without destroying human and natural resources in the process? At an Appalachian city that rose during the early 1940's as if by magic along the Black Oak Ridge in Tennessee there were unlocked secrets of the universe previously unknown to humans. It defies the history of human ingenuity to claim that lesser problems cannot be overcome.

People living in the Appalachian ranges —from the rocky promontories where the mountains meet the sea on Gaspé to the dense highlands of Georgia's Brasstown Bald and Alabama's Little Alps—have been overcoming obstacles for a long time. Historian James Truslow Adams asserted that in New England's harsh weather and rocky soil "the gristle of conscience, work, thrift, shrewdness, duty, become bone." With gristle and bone watered by sweat they cleared the fields and laid up stone walls whose firm outline stitches together many a patchwork of farms and boundaries today. They built strong bridges covered with sound timbers and their beautiful utility still delights us.

In the central and southern Appala-

chians, too, there was the stern credo of "make, make-do, or do without." The settlers needed shelters and they hewed out sturdy cabins of logs notched and matched, roof shingles rived in the right time of the moon. They needed utensils and they wove baskets from tough white-oak splits and honeysuckle vines colored with dyes drawn from root and bark; they whittled churns from sweet-smelling cedar, shaped pots from native clay, and dolls and other play-pretties from cornshucks. They needed sweets and in New England they boiled the syrup of the maple tree to drench their flapjacks and in the south they robbed wild bee gums of sourwood honey to cover their biscuits. They wanted music and they made dulcimers. And all through the Appalachians they thirsted for something to quicken their pulses and their Saturday pleasure and they distilled applejack and rye and corn, any fruit or grain that was handy, but especially corn. It was a tax on their whiskey, proposed by that friend of the eastern bankers, Alexander Hamilton, that led to rebellion in the western mountains soon after the birth of the new republic, a rebellion put down only after President George Washington led federal troops into the Alleghenies. Resistance to the tax was stifled—but not the suspicion of the Appalachian Mountain dwellers toward their eastern leaders.

Philadelphia's urbane lawyer Gouvernor Morris gave voice in 1787 to the attitudes of many of the settled east coast gentry when he complained, "I dread the cold and sower temper of the back counties."

The temper might have been less "sower" if mutual distrust concerning land boundaries had been diminished. Mountain people had reason to be cantankerous about questions of land. Conflicting colonial grants and the conniving of speculators led to early disputes over land ownership. Thus Daniel Boone, whose family had followed the Great Valley from Pennsylvania through Virginia into North Carolina, who blazed the Wilderness Road through Cumberland Gap for thousands of settlers to the rich canebrakes and meadows and salt licks of Kentucky, found himself in old age displaced from acres he thought he owned, seeking new land to call home.

Scarcely one of the original 13 colonies escaped some friction, during or following

Logger totes pails of springwater back to his cabin deep in wilderness area of the Green Mountains in Vermont. Camp is accessible only by canoe on wild and turbulent Black Branch of the Nulhegan River.

the Revolutionary War, with its neighbors or among its own citizens over the question of western boundaries. Conflict between Connecticut and Pennsylvania over lands along the Susquehanna led to a series of three engagements that came to be known as the Pennymite Wars, and at the height of the colonial struggle for survival one military leader bitterly observed, "Pennsylvania and New England troops would as soon fight each other as the enemy." During the Revolution, in 1777, rocky Vermont culminated years of hostility with New York and New Hampshire over land claims by declaring its independence. During the next 14 years Vermont survived, weak but stubbornly quarrelsome with its larger neighbors until limits were finally set and it became the 14th sate in the Union in 1791. Its constitution was the first in America to outlaw all slavery and grant universal suffrage to all men regardless of their economic status. (No mention was made of women.)

The issue of slavery brought into sharp focus the differences between southern state governments and their Appalachian Mountain counties. Mountain land was usually poorer land than that farmed by lowland planters. Slaves were not part of the economy of tilted pastures and garden-plots. But the taxation and suffrage laws of the southern states benefitted those who held slaves as part of their "property." When the Civil War erupted many mountain people grumbled that it was a rich man's war and a poor man's fight.

There were also genuine anti-slavery

sentiments in the Appalachian Mountains. In the shadow of the Unakas the first newspaper in the United States to advocate emancipation began publication in 1819. Anti-slavery feeling was so strong in one area of northern Alabama that in 1861, at the beginning of the war, formation of a new pro-Union state was proposed. It was to be called Nickajack, probably for the famous cave at the dangerous Suck or Boiling Pot of the Tennessee River where fierce Indian guerillas had attacked early settlers and raftsmen using the waterway.

Efforts to bring Nickajack into being were aborted but determination to bring a new western state out of Virginia's Appalachians was successful. Defiance that had built up for years against the Old Dominion came to open revolt in 1861. When secession from the Union was ratified by Virginia its western counties decided to

Fisherman attempting to prove the worth of his lures in Loyalsock Creek, originating in Pennsylvania's mountain region. This gin clear stream attracts numerous anglers.

secede from Virginia. Two years later President Lincoln issued a proclamation that made the Mountain State, West Virginia, the 35th of the Union.

In Appalachian counties of North Carolina and Tennessee there was talk of secession. More important, there was strong support for the Union cause. North Carolina sent more than 8,000 soldiers into Federal lines, while Tennessee sent more than 50,000. On her official quota alone (over 31,000 soldiers) Tennessee provided more Federal troops than Rhode Island or Delaware and almost as many as New Hampshire or Vermont.

The Appalachian Valley was crucial to the waging of the Civil War. In the broad fields and rolling hills of the Valley of

Virginia and the Tennessee Valley, troops of the blue and gray played hide and seek and clashed in some of the costliest engagements of that conflict, from blood-stained patches of earth known as the Peach Orchard and the Wheat Field and Devil's Den on the Cumberland Valley battleground of Gettysburg to the battle fought above the clouds on Chattanooga's Lookout Mountain. Cumberland Gap was a strategic gateway to the South and on its jutting summit and among its woods contests for control see-sawed back and forth from Federal to Confederate victory.

Throughout the war the southern mountains were laced with trails over which Union sympathizers pushed north to join the U.S. army. Federal prisoners fleeing from the south could also find friendly guides through this difficult terrain. The mountain men who led recruits or escapees through the hazards of the trails came to be known as pilots. Often their dedication was more to an individual who needed their help than to political allegiance to either army.

The name of one Appalachian village is forever associated with the man whose actions foreshadowed the bloodbath of war. In 1859 Harpers Ferry was an industrial village perched above the confluence of the Potomac and Shenandoah rivers in the Blue Ridge Mountains of Virginia. On a rainy night in October John Brown and 19 followers marched on foot and by wagon from Maryland to sieze the Harpers Ferry United States arsenal. They surprised the guard and entered the armory where Brown issued a warning: "I came here from Kansas, and this is a slave state; I want to free all the Negroes in this state. I have possession now of the United States armory, and if the citizens interfere with me I must only burn the town and have blood."

In possession of the armory Brown's little band held out against siege by the local militia until a U.S. Lieutenant Colonel, Robert E. Lee, arrived with 90 Marines and captured Brown and six of his men. Two of Brown's sons were killed.

John Brown was tried and hanged in the city of Charlestown, which would later become the capital of the new state of West Virginia. Terror inspired by the raid helped silence the voices of reason trying to be heard above the shouts of those tense

Docile face of young white tail deer on Grandfather Mountain in North Carolina.

years. Brown had helped fulfill his own dark prophecy stated in a note he handed one of his guards before the execution. " I, John Brown," he wrote, "am now quite certain that the crimes of this guilty land: will never be purged away; but with blood."

It was a terrible purging. A Northern journalist traveling through the southern Appalachian Mountains at the close of the Civil War found Harpers Ferry a desolate place. "Freshets tear down the streets, and the dreary hillsides present only ragged weeds. The town itself lies half in ruins." Farther down the Appalachians, at the site of a bitter engagement on Missionary Ridge near Chattanooga, the traveler found a grisly sight: "Through woods dotted with the graves of soldiers buried where they fell, we drove to the scene of that final fight. Bones of dead horses strewed the ground. At the foot of the wooded hill were trenches full of Longstreet's slaughtered men . . . cut down like ripe grain by the deadly volleys which poured from a crescent of flame and smoke, where the heroic remnant of the army had taken up its position and was not to be dislodged."

Scarred and impoverished the Appalachian Mountain region survived the war to begin a long new cycle of scarring and exploitation—this time by industries, some of them already mentioned, and by the well-intentioned as well as the mischief-makers who brought their own plan of "development" for land and people.

The remains of wars, of explorations, of nature's mysteries and people's adventures lie scattered across the Appalachians. Among the most unyielding mysteries are those that are among the oldest. These are the undeciphered stones: standing, bal-

anced, perched, piled, inscribed, aligned, distributed from Alabama to northern Canada. Their various formations zig zag across hill tops, sprawl on ice-scarred pinnacles, rest in quiet woods, rise along steep slopes. What was their purpose? Who fashioned them, and when? Mute and mysterious in Coffee County, Tennessee, or Putnam County, New York, in Vermont or West Virginia or dozens of other sites, they remind us that people have been in these old hills for longer than we may suspect. Incisions on one of the largest single standing stones, near South Royalton, Vermont, have been dismissed as "glacial scratchings" and hailed as "the organized symbols of an as yet undetermined script." Scattered in the forest around Mahopac, N.Y. are "scores of corbelled, long-barrowed chambers." Can these be explained as root cellars of early settlers, or dwellings of "freed New England slaves," or ancient Celtic structures? These and other origins have been supported by various bits' of evidence. Are the inscriptions on a stone tablet found in West Virginia more than a century ago of Celtic influence? Some scholars believe so. Was the Old Stone Fort in Tennessee for ancient ceremonial use—and what was the nature of the rituals? Neither archaeology nor legend has answered the riddle as yet. Out of some distant dawn these unexplained forts and monuments and inscriptions arise and leave us without translations of their message or their meaning, leave us with wonder.

Wonder—at nature's infinite variety, at human responses to that variety—may be the emotion most common among those who have sought to suck the very marrow of an Appalachian experience. Two quite opposite groups of "explorers" have been touched by this wonder: those who hike along the crests and among the valleys on the Appalachian Trail and those remarkable artists whose vision and canvasses represent the only "art school" America has ever harbored.

The Appalachian Trail was Benton Mac-Kaye's brain child. The "longest marked continuous footpath in the world," it reaches some 2,000 miles from Mt. Katahdin in central Maine to Springer Mountain in northern Georgia. Begun in 1922 in New York it passes through 14 states and except

for a northern portion parallels the Great Indian Warpath. It is tended by the Appalachian Trail Conference, made up of volunteer groups and individuals coordinating state and federal efforts with their own. Primitive shelters and rough markers dot the trail. Along the way nature poses tests of character, stamina, and ingenuity in rough terrain, searing heat, sudden snowfall. History comes alive as a hiker's footsteps find their way along old Indian paths, lumber trails, charcoal-pit roads, forgotten mining routes, stage coach lanes, livestock runs, and beds of early railroads—all part of the Appalachian Trail. And how many have shouted the joy of that final push through cruel Mahoosuc Notch, across the Maine wilderness, and finally, "The top. The top of Mt. Katahdin! I made it!"

Uniquely, perhaps, we find a group of painters, the Hudson River School of the 19th Century, offering profound insights into all that we have discussed in these pages relating to the past, present and future of the Appalachian Mountains. These artists' perceptions encompassed the varied natural world of the Appalachians as well as the variety of human responses evoked by nature's challenge, responses ranging from the romantically sublime to the blindly commercial. To know the greatest of these artists, who are now enjoying an animated revival after decades of neglect, is to know a kind of mountaintop ending of Appalachian awareness.

Late in the 1820's the English immigrant Thomas Cole, who had helped his parents engrave wallpaper designs and had done portraits and commercial paintings in various cities before moving to New York, made sketches in the Catskill Mountains of what was still wilderness scenery. Displaying his finished paintings in the city, he attracted famous artists and business patrons and became America's first great landscape painter.

Cole's love of nature adapted well to the theory of landscape painting current in England and America at the time, which was to create feelings in the viewer of the beautiful or the sublime. A dramatic foreground drew the viewer into the work and a massive object in the distance focused interest within it. Cole normally used a twisted dead tree at the side of his foreground and, as the focal point, such natural phenomena as Oxbow River as seen from the Berkshires for the peaceful painting or the Kaaterskill Falls in the Catskills for the sublime. Cole's expression of nature, especially through his use of light, which could be either highly realistic or inventive and dramatic—as in a painting he called The Course of Empire—made him a truly original landscape artist.

The second painter of the Hudson River School was Asher Durand. A well-known engraver of American money and a portraitist, in 1836 he decided to join Cole in the wilderness and try his hand at landscapes. Instead of exaggerating nature as Cole did, Durand tried to show that natural scenes in themselves had an epic quality and that a person's life in nature was itself an epic. In The Indian's Vespers of 1847 an Indian gazes worshipfully at the sky and distant vista beyond a lake at sunset. The Indian and the massive trees with long roots in the foreground were emblematic of the wilderness to Durand, who realized it was disappearing.

To better convey distance in these panoramas he experimented with a vertical format and used this under unusual circumstances in 1849 to create a painting with an Appalachian Mountain setting and literary-artistic history. The artist Cole had died and his patron, Sturges, after hearing William Cullen Bryant's moving oration on Cole's death, commissioned from Durand a painting of the poet and Cole together. Durand entitled it Kindred Spirits after the Keats sonnet with the theme of two kindred spirits meeting in the wilderness. Durand places the artist with sketch pad and poet with cane overlooking Cole's favorite area, the valley of the Kaaterskill Falls, with high banks, rocky cliffs and several of Cole's own "storm-blasted" trees falling toward the stream. Within this "wild scene" (as a reviewer called it) the pair stand on a rocky bluff with Cole lecturing to Bryant about the view. Their initials carved on a nearby tree bear witness to their communion with nature. Height of the cliffs imparts grandeur to the scene.

With Cole's allegories, landscapes were gradually being accepted in America as having a moral purpose and Durand's tall landscapes of trees seemed to follow this trend, reflecting the awe that Appalachian mountains had inspired since aboriginal

times. Durand's In the Woods stirred its owner, a reverend, to the feeling of being in "a majestic cathedral wherein to extemporize Te Deums and High Masses at my own sweet will."

Durand also developed imaginary landscapes and Biblical subjects and allegory as in Landscape, Progress. In this, a group of Indians in a wilderness of massive rocks and trees look down upon a plain dotted with pioneer homesteads and a herd of cattle. Stretching from the houses is a lake or river with a steamboat arriving and a railroad and a canal following the water into the distance. Durand clearly proclaims his belief in America's manifest destiny at the same time as the wilderness was being pushed beyond Appalachia into the western states.

Durand used effectively the tree stump and ax-felled tree which have been described recently as important symbols in American art of the last century. Certainly they were important to an understanding of the Appalachians. As settlements and towns grew (with industries such as charcoal-making gulping thousands of cords of wood) forests were decimated. There are more trees in New England today than remained by 1850. The towering trees that appeared in Durand's wilderness scenes before 1850 were seldom seen after that.

In both his mountain and pastoral scenes, however, Durand showed that nature remains abundant even though civilization advances upon it. In his Landscape with Vista, at a stream's edge a huge tree with long roots, reminder of wilderness, grasps toward the water while cows drink from the stream, suggesting that human activity still depends on water from the wilderness.

But Durand's renditions became too dependent upon popular demand. He, too, began to alter nature. Recognizable mountains remained in the background but the foreground became "woodland" scenes relaxing the viewer or "flat" scenes of meadows in keeping with the vogue for Dutch paintings. In Catskill Clove of 1866 Durand did return to long vistas of mountains seen from the edge of the wilderness, painted perhaps not just as a mountain scene but as a symbolic reminder that America could regain through nature the unity lost in the Civil War.

Durand's nostalgia was echoed by Frederic Church, another follower of Cole, who combined the romantic view of nature with a scientific style. In the 1850's in addition to depicting mountains such as Maine's Katahdin he made oil sketches of crashing surf and jagged rocks along the coast. This led him to Newfoundland where he examined the strange shapes and light effects of icebergs—and created a work that would bring in 1979 one of the highest prices ever paid for any painting. His last mountain painting of the decade was Twilight in the Wilderness of 1860. After the death of a child, Church travelled to Jamaica to paint tropical foliage which he combined with rolling mountains of that island. Like Church, Durand saw the

Covered bridge and small church are long-standing structures revered and enjoyed by the residents of Stark, New Hampshire. This small village is nestled within the rugged Pilot Range and White Mountains.

wilderness as the repose of a merciful nature but unlike him Durand continued to look for it in the Appalachian Mountains.

But the wilderness changed and the approach was now the idea of the scenic. This was a vital shift in attitude, significant not only to art but as a reflection of public escape from the hard challenges of America's land and resources realities to pretty and undemanding unreality.

Jasper Cropsey, an architect who became a painter of the scenery around the Hudson River and in New England, was generally further away from Cole's unspoiled wilderness than was Durand even though he looked to the same mountains. He believed that nature as shown in art should serve the picturesque. About the middle of his seven year stay in England from 1856 to 1863 he used sketches brought from America for a painting that made him famous in England as well as America, Autumn on the Hudson. Cropsey created a vast panoramic scene which somewhat imitated The Heart of the Andes by Church. Church had shown three different Andes environments within the same retreating space; tropical lowlands in front, rugged hills in the middle, snow-covered peaks in the background. Within each environment Church had crammed so much detail that the crowds who came to see it used opera glasses or tin tubes Church provided to view each segment separately, and Church was regarded as having presented nature as a scientific phenomenon in the manner of von Homboldt, the German naturalist.

Cropsey adopted Church's idea of a panorama of detail in three areas. There is wilderness, a forest, a pool surrounded by boulders, dead logs and trees with autumn foliage. The wilderness turns into a grassy slope with a stream and cattle drinking. In the distance are tiny houses of the towns of Newburgh, New Windsor and West Point. Around the shore a promontory of the Hudson Highlands closes off the bay. Beyond this promontory is the distant shore with clouds, all bathed by light from the sun high in the sky.

While the English audience would have noticed the wilderness foreground with brilliant autumn foliage, an American would have noticed the effects of human treatment upon nature in keeping with current ideas of the picturesque. In 1850 the writer Nathaniel Willis, foreshadowing generations of Appalachian land promoters to follow, composed an essay eulogizing "The Highland Terrace above West Point" as a place for wealthy city dwellers to move to: it conformed to the picturesque ideal and the city was only a few hours away by steamship or locomotive. This ten mile square of land could be the same ledge viewed in Cropsey's painting.

Tall dramatic mountains appear in Cropsey's Starrucca Viaduct which shows the new railroad bridge overlooking the Susquehanna Valley in Pennsylvania. A train is crossing the bridge between two mountains; several people sit on a rock admiring the train. There is colorful autumn foliage and a picturesque mill, houses, and wooden bridge. The focus

of interest, however, is in the new technology, the train and its bridge. Cropsey seems to suggest that these objects are picturesque in their own way. They will conquer the wilderness—the steam of the train engine rises up to meet the mist and the railroad tracks have sliced the mountainsides and driven a wedge through the wilderness.

But Cropsey did not continue to explore such examples of American progress. His later works keep man-made sights limited to those associated with charm and venerability. By Cropsey's time the artists themselves had helped render the wilderness picturesque. In New Hampshire a waterfalls was renamed Artists' Falls. Inns were made famous by their artist patrons.

In contrast to Cropsey, the painter George Inness immediately perceived the relationship between the wilderness and the modern industrial world, and expressed it in the panoramic style of Cole and Durand, in The Lackawanna Valley of 1855, which the Erie Railroad had commissioned as a view of their new station, and in several paintings of the Delaware Water Gap around 1860. Inness perceived the drama of the modern world in nature but as yet refused to comment upon it.

By the end of the nineteenth century American painting was dominated by classical mural paintings for vast architectural schemes, by social realism of the emerging slums, and by meditative fantasies inspired by the Symbolist art of Europe. It was only when artists began to look with realism and imagination at the total American landscape that they achieved once more the insights of the Hudson River School painters.

During the 1920's, at the same time as he studied the houses and streets of American cities and towns, Charles Burchfield observed the natural world of trees and plants as they encroached on man's farms and roads, and the vibrant light and air which affected both the natural objects and the man-made structures and eroded hills in nature. Often painting in or near the Appalachians, he gained, as had the Hudson River artists, a vision of America itself by painting in these mountains. In deciding to paint natural forms instead of just the factories and railroads which dominated the landscape, Burchfield began to

Dwarf cinquefoil Potentilla roffinsiana in White Mountains of New Hampshire. This rare plant is the size of a half-dollar, found only on Mt. Washington above timberline.

comprehend the living vibrancy of nature as Durand had understood earlier. But he perceived nature as vibrating in all her seasons, not just in Durand's summer greenery, and in all types of suburban landscapes, not just the wilderness.

They preserved a vision of the Appalachian wilderness, those Hudson River painters, even as they transformed it. Such has been the ironic story of the Appalachians and human history.

The Appalachians have received them all: Spanish conquistadores, Scotch-Irish traders, rovers and settlers, lumbermen and botanists, artists and industrialists, the makers of war and keepers of peace, the caretakers and the careless. Each made individual response to this ancient and varied land, each left some mark upon it.

The question now is, what shall be our response to this paradoxically fragile and indomitable land? Author Alf Evers has said, "among the mountains, two powerful sides of life have operated side by side and, by a thousand strokes, given the region its shape. One was the greed for land and wealth and the power over others which both symbolize; the other was the free play of the imagination in the arts and in the exploration of nature. Sometimes the two forces worked together, more often they were locked in battle."

To behold and cherish the beauty of the Appalachian Mountains, to bring forth and use the wealth of the Appalachians wisely, this calls for power and imagination working together, not locked in battle. It is a challenge as enduring and noble as the ancient Appalachians themselves.

Mist from Desoto Falls in Alabama's Little River Gorge clings to foliage along canyon wall.

Cotton boll ready for harvest is indicative of numerous cotton fields surrounding tip of southern Appalachians near Piedmont, Alabama. Right: Road to summit of 2,719 foot Mt. Cheaha, highest point in Alabama renders pleasant view of trailing end of Appalachian Mountain Range.

Low hanging clouds blanket mountain in Chattahoochee National Forest, merging with moisture rising from surface of small lake in late November. Numerous lakes prevail in this region. Left: Golden light of dawn silhouettes a group of pines along shore of Lake Chatuge near Hiawassee, Georgia.

Autumn colors embellish wooded area on the slopes of Brasstown Bald, Georgia's highest mountain. Right: Intimate detail of morning glory blossom thrusts its brilliant beauty on the beholder. Pages 40 and 41 following: Setting sun drifting below crest of ridge in Great Smoky Mountains of North Carolina.

View from Point Park atop
Lookout Mountain defines
Moccasin Bend of Tennessee
River and city of Chattanooga
where key battle of Civil War
was waged. Left: Chattooga
River leaving headwaters in
North Carolina, twists and
turns through gorge of un-
usual beauty. Pages 44 and 45
following: Hikers pause for
study of Tennessee on Charlie's
Bunion along Appalachian
Trail in Great Smoky Mountains.

Well proportioned maple tree enhances the natural beauty of Cades Cove in Great Smoky Mountains of Tennessee. Right: From summit of Roan Mountain near North Carolina border the Southern Appalachians appear endless as they penetrate deep into Tennessee.

Forested slopes of the Great Smoky Mountains National Park offer a relaxing period, away from our daily chores. Left: Farmer at work in rocky soil near Newdale, North Carolina. Farming steep hillsides of this region demands agility, plus special plow which turns furrows out and a horse void of fear at these elevations.

Yellow poplars, stately monarchs in Joyce Kilmer National Memorial Forest, North Carolina average five to six feet in diameter and approximately 500 years old. Right: Aerial view reveals a sea of clouds hugging mountain elevations along the great Tennessee, North Carolina divide.

Moss and lichen adhere to gnarled oak close to summit of Big Yellow Bald near Newland, North Carolina. Left: Segment of the Appalachian Trail that straddles the North Carolina, Tennessee state line, traversed by countless hikers. It exceeds 2,000 miles in length, from Maine to Georgia.

Spring greens of dog hobble
drape over wild flowers
in sylvan glade, distinct area of
Blue Ridge Mountains, North
Carolina. Left: Gentle flow of
tiny brook is indicative of mood
surrounding Banner Elk, North
Carolina. Pages 60 and 61
following: Grassy Balds are
unexplainable feature of southern Appalachian summits.
View from Little Bald Mountain
into North Carolina as the
tussocks grow golden at sunrise.

Numerous cabbage patches dot crest of Blue Ridge Mountains in North Carolina. Right: Humpback Mountain overlooks Linville Gorge from Blue Ridge Parkway near Spruce Pine, North Carolina.

Weather-worn tree reflects the will to survive under wretched conditions on slope of Big Bald Mountain, North Carolina. Left: Winter's limited mantle livens view of Grandfather Mountain from summit of Sugar Mountain, North Carolina.

Summits of the Blue Ridge Mountains form an incredible exposure near Sylva, North Carolina. Right: Fringed phacelia, indigenous to the Southern Appalachians, whitens the forest floor in April and May.

Crabtree Meadow Falls near Little Switzerland on Blue Ridge Parkway, North Carolina. Left: Lavish display of vaseyi (vaz-e-i) blossoms, member of Azalea family, at Grandfather Mountain, North Carolina.

Segment of Blue Ridge Parkway reveals sampling of nature, extending 469 miles along crest of Southern Appalachians in North Carolina and Virginia. Right: Spike-like cluster of galax blossoms signify one additional wild flower indigenous to the Southern Appalachians. Pages 72 and 73 following: Hardwood tree frames 3,268 foot Old Rag Mountain in Shenandoah National Park, gift to the nation from the people of Virginia.

Shenandoah Valley from Blue
Ridge Mountains of Virginia.
View is from crest of breathtaking Skyline Drive. Left: Old
tobacco storage cabin made
of logs and chinked with
red clay, in southern Virginia.
Pages 76 and 77 following:
From summit of Sugar Mountain
near Banner Elk, North Carolina, spectacular panorama
unfolds in Pisgah National
Forest. Peak on right is 6,684
foot Mt. Mitchell, highest elevation in Appalachian chain.

Water wheel, sign of a bygone era, is still functional at Mabry Mill, Virginia on the Blue Ridge Parkway. Right: Ripples momentarily disturb surface of mountain pond in George Washington National Forest of Virginia.

Rafters plunge into hydraulic on West Virginia's New River. Boiling rapids pass through canyon below world's highest and longest single arch steel bridge. Left: Frontier cabin deep in hollow of the Virginia mountains.

In October berries of dogwood
trees revert to bright red.
Right: Spruce trees on Cheat
Mountain mark site of Snow-
shoe ski run near Slaty Fork,
West Virginia. Dense forest of
conifers prevailed here at turn
of century.

Restored house at Harpers Ferry, West Virginia. Heart of community has been designated National Historical Park and continues to undergo extensive restoration. Left: Dogwood blossoms at their peak along Skyline Drive, Shenandoah National Park, Virginia.

Sunlight maximizes beauty of sundrop blossom in Mononga-hela National Forest, West Virginia. Right: Seneca Rocks, a jagged, challenging sand-stone formation for climbers in heart of North Fork Mountain, West Virginia. Pages 88 and 89 following: Cattle in foreground, reflect the peace and serenity that prevails amidst final resting place of early pioneers near Burkittsville, Maryland.

Harpers Ferry, West Virginia
situated on point of land at
confluence of Potomac and
Shenandoah Rivers. Spire at left
identifies St. Peter's Catholic
Church, erected in 1830s and
later remodeled, still in use
today. Left: Black-eyed Susan
blossoms a favorite member of
the sunflower family. Pages
92 and 93 following: Silent glow
of winter surrounds bridge
that spans partially frozen creek
near Osteberg, Pennsylvania.

Moisture-laden crocus in early morning on mountain slope in Pennsylvania. Right: Skeletal remains of a once proud barn under a brooding sky, in Endless Mountain region of Pennsylvania.

Minute details are always expressed in the numerous ferns that dot the landscape of this great country. Left: Signs of winter prevail along shore of creek in the Pocono Mountains of Pennsylvania.

Flowering tree on hillside in the Allegheny National Forest of Pennsylvania. Right: Lake Jean at dawn on western edge of Ricketts Glen State Park near Red Rock, Pennsylvania.

Horses satisfy their hunger on a gentle slope above the Susquehanna River at Lauxmont Farms near Wrightsville, Pennsylvania. Left: Pine Creek flows deep within Pennsylvania's Grand Canyon near Wellsboro.

Memorial monument erected on the summit of 1,803 foot High Point. It is the highest elevation in New Jersey, rendering a commanding view of Kittatinny Mountains. Right: Delaware River flows between Pennsylvania and New Jersey at Delaware Water Gap National Recreation Area. Pages 104 and 105 following: Grass carpets many areas of the Appalachian Mountains, firmly anchoring the soil to prevent erosion.

Mohonk Mountain House straddles Shawangunk Mountains with commanding view of the Catskills. In foreground glacial lake abuts enormous granite cliffs. Right: A pleasant change of pace awaits the traveler at Wells Bridge, New York. Pages 108 and 109 following: Light dusting of snow signals the arrival of winter on crest of Catskill Mountains in New York. View is toward a shoulder of 3,990 ft. Black Dome Mountain.

Intimate view of willow leaves encrusted with barbs of frost crystals. Left: Maximum thrust of winter is evident in dense forest of Catskill Mountains.

Shawangunk Mountains of New York lift eastward toward the Hudson River Valley. Right: Fishermen enjoy a balmy fall day on the Housatonic River near Cornwall, Connecticut.

Dense grove of white birch in Berkshire Mountains of Massachusetts. Left: Reflection on pond in Housatonic State Forest near Cornwall Bridge, Connecticut.

Natural beauty abounds in the Berkshire region that spans extreme western sector of Massachusetts. Right: Pond at the base of 3,491 foot Mt. Greylock, highest point in Massachusetts.

Young girl studies intricate details of wildflowers along a back road in Vermont. Left: Children in the community of Newark, Vermont still enjoy the educational facilities of the historic one-room red schoolhouse. In distance shoulder of Burke Mountain. Pages 120 and 121 following: Western flank of Mt. Mansfield in the Green Mountains looking east from Underhill, Vermont.

Storm clouds swirl over Camels Hump in Green Mountains of Vermont. Right: Magnificent sugar maple dressed in autumn splendor along shore of the Connecticut River near Guild-hill, Vermont. Pages 124 and 125 following: Field of daisies in Vermont, bares the beauty of natures handiwork.

View from 4,393 foot Mt. Mansfield, Vermont's highest peak. Adirondack Mountains of New York state resemble saw-tooth rib over Lake Champlain. Left: Canoeist threads his way between huge boulders on the New Haven River near Bristol, Vermont. Spring thaws on many state streams offer rousing challenge to boaters.

Stearling Pond, shelter on crest of Green Mountains, Vermont. Trail stretching from Massachusetts to Canada has several similar shelters strategically located for hikers' convenience. Right: Void of fear, entrant challenges her adversaries in annual freestyle aerial competition at Stowe, Vermont.

Snow blankets Mt. Mansfield
providing near-perfect alpine
terrain for skiers. World famous
Stowe Ski area is on its eastern
slope. Left: Homes in Pleasant
Valley seemingly hug the
ascending face of Mt. Mansfield, near Underhill, Vermont.

Small dairy farms are numerous
in number on the rolling hills
and verdant pasture areas
across Vermont. Right: Beauty
of cherry blossoms remains
unmatched when they burst
forth in rural Vermont.

Sap buckets on sugar maples is familiar spring sight in Green Mountains of Vermont. This well-maintained farm is near Woodstock. Left: Unmatched beauty of autumn foliage portends the arrival of winter in hardwood forest of Vermont. Pages 136 and 137 following: Headwall of Tuckerman Ravine is example of New England's finest glacial cirque. Snow depth in bowl extends ski season into spring.

Old Man of the Mountains natural formation in Franconia Notch, symbol of New Hampshire. Left: View from summit of Mt. Washington looks over Boott Spur. This day the wind peaked at 121 miles per hour and temperature registered 24 degrees below zero. Pages 140 and 141 following: Ridges of Presidential Range in New Hampshire where chill factor can sometimes reach 100 degrees below zero. Many lives of ill-prepared have perished here.

Mt. Washington Weather Observatory in a fierce blizzard. On this site the highest natural wind velocity ever recorded by man reached 231 miles per hour, April 12, 1934. Right: Mountaineers descend from Mt. Lincoln, on the Franconia Range in White Mountains of northern New Hampshire.

Hikers meditate on their achievement atop Bondcliff, hidden away in Pemigewasset Wilderness of the White Mountains. Left: Diapensia, carpets a near-summit area of Mt. Washington. In distance, Mt. Madison and Mt. Adams, second highest peak in White Mountains of New Hampshire.

Climbers ascend headwall of King Ravine on north side of 5,798 foot Mt. Adams in Presidential Range, New Hampshire. Right: Eagle Cliff soars above Profile Lake in Franconia Notch, New Hampshire.

Waning autumn foliage heralds
the coming of winter on rural
road near Greenville, Maine.
Left: Initial thrust of winter
appears on forest of evergreens
in northern Maine.

Bull moose stands in the Allagash River, Maine. This river was the first to be incorporated in National Wild and Scenic Rivers System. Right: Rare view of our national symbol, the bald eagle, observed in wilderness area of northern Maine. Pages 152 and 153 following: Storm clouds sweep across rugged slopes of 5,268 foot Mt. Katahdin, highest elevation in Maine. It is northern terminal of Appalachian Trail.

Dense stand of gray birch makes an imposing forest in the Bigelow Range. Left: Red sunrise along the St. John River aptly forecasts a day of rain. Lakes and intricate waterways prevail throughout a major portion of Maine. Pages 156 and 157 following. Voyagers paddle misty waters of Umsaskis Lake on Maine's Allagash Wilderness Waterway.

Oxen pulling stone drag
(sometimes called stoneboat)
to break clods at L. R. Toleman
farm near Winthrop, Maine.
Right: Brilliant autumns so
famous in New England are
aided by chilly nights and
sun-warmed days.

APPALACHIAN MOUNTAINS

I first became acquainted with the Appalachian Mountains in the year 1933. It began in early April when a young fire warden and his wife were laboring up a snow-choked mountain trail in central New Hampshire. They trudged along on snowshoes and each carried a heavy pack-basket. Winter's accumulation of snow had nearly all melted in the valleys below, but up on the mountain it was a different story. The spring thaw was underway. Rivulets and small streams undermined the snow pack creating unseen pockets into which the snowshoers would flounder, sometimes up to their hips. It was an exhausting way to climb a mountain.

After many hours of struggle they reached a tiny one room cabin at the edge of treeline. It was just a short distance from the mountain's summit where a firetower perched on top. For the fire warden and his wife this small cabin would be home for the next nine years! They took off their pack-baskets and collapsed on the cabin's porch. One of the pack-baskets began to wiggle, and a two-year-old boy popped his head up to look around! That youngster was me, and from that moment I began a unique life of living and growing with nature on top of my first Appalachian Mountain.

The mountain is called Cardigan. A mere 3,121 feet above sea level. Not much when one considers the big peaks of our country's far west, but for Easterners the Appalachian Mountains have their own special prominence. The valleys are much closer to sea level and the peaks themselves, being geographically older, are more rounded. I like to think of the mountains as being friendlier. Cardigan's smooth, rocky summit is one of those, standing high above the surrounding countryside with an unrestricted view, making it an ideal spot for a firetower.

I often thought of it as Blueberry Mountain, for its ledges were covered with little islands of wild blueberry bushes. In summer swarms of people would come up the mountain with buckets, cans, tins and containers of all sorts to pick the delicious berries. My mother and I would scour the mountain during berry season picking quart after quart which we would carry down to sell at summer resorts in the valley below. We would eat blueberries until they came out our ears, and believe me, back in those days just after the Depression, we were thankful to supplement our diet in any way we could. My father's pay as a firelookout was pretty slim but it was far better than no job at all.

We also had a small garden at our cabin. Soil had to be carried up on our backs a half-mile over the ledges. The same with our firewood, and in dry times, our drinking water, too. All our food supplies had to be packed from a parking lot a mile and a half away. The nearest house was more than three miles—that's where we got our milk and eggs. In later years we brought up a couple of chickens so we didn't have to go quite so far for eggs.

The adventures of my boyhood on the mountain could fill volumes. The experiences of wild electric storms including several which demolished the tower and struck the cabin are fused within my memory! We even survived the great hurricane of 1938, when for the grace of two enormous chains which circled the cabin roof, we would have surely been whisked off the mountain in winds over 100 miles per hour! There were snow storms and blizzards in April and May, then later in October and November just before we moved off the mountain for winter season. (There was no fire danger in winter, of course, so the lookout's job was suspended during these months.)

I learned about wildlife early, meeting all kinds of black bears, wildcats, lynx, deer, foxes and porcupines. Porkeys were quite prevalent and provided my first source of income. There was a bounty on them in those days because the critters destroyed so many trees by girdling its bark. New Hampshire Town Selectmen were instructed to pay 20 cents for every porkey nose brought in. As a youngster I tried to capitalize on this windfall but I was seldom a match for the tough little porkey who could scramble out on the skinniest limb in the highest tree. If I made a dollar during the entire season I was doing well.

Going to school was a major undertaking since it was 3½ miles of hiking one way. No bus service for me on the mountain and I had to trudge the trail daily, rain or shine. In spring it often meant wearing snowshoes and floundering in rotten snow undermined by meltwater. By the time I reached school I was usually a soaking mess. Snowshoes and a pack with my lunch were standard procedure for my early education.

The school was a classic one-room building with eight grades and one teacher. Besides readin' writin' and 'rithmetic, we all had to share in chores at school, such as getting in firewood, sweeping floors and bringing in springwater from a flowing pipe up a slippery hillside path. Oldest boys were responsible for splitting firewood while the rest of us took turns stoking our one big potbelly stove.

After school I still had the long walk by myself back up the mountain. Three and one-half miles for a small boy with short legs seemed like forever, especially if it was raining and cold. I often arrived back at the cabin after dark. It was during some of those dreary hours at just about dusk when I would have my most frightening moment. Two little screech owls would team up in a tree right over the trail and blast out a blood curdling scream. I never knew which tree they would be in and they seemed to delight in scaring the pants off me!

Cardigan became a base camp for further exploration into New Hampshire's White Mountains during my growing years. My father had an affinity for trails and was especially interested in the Appalachian Trail. At the age of four I climbed Mt. Washington, the highest peak in New England, along with my parents. From that point on there was no stopping me and I accompanied my father to the summits of most all major mountains in Maine, New Hampshire and Vermont.

Toward the end of nine years on Mt. Cardigan, my father took a Park Service examination and we moved to North Carolina during the Second World War where he was assigned as a Ranger on the Blue Ridge Parkway. I continued on through high school and also pursued exploration of the Southern Appalachians in parts of Virginia, North Carolina and Tennessee. It was a whole new world with many more mountain peaks to discover.

In summer I returned to my home state of New Hampshire where I was a counselor at a boys' camp in charge of its trip department. My familiarity with the New England mountains was a big asset in providing an active outdoor program for the camp over a many year period. Mt. Cardigan was nearby and I took every opportunity to revisit my old stomping grounds and familiar territory.

In retrospect, the spirit of the Appalachian Mountains is in my blood running wild and free. The spark was ignited the day my folks plunked that pack-basket down on the cabin porch and I became part of those friendly mountains. In all the years of many wanderings to great mountains in far away lands, the Appalachians have always drawn me back. For me they are ever irresistible. I owe a good deal to my parents and the circumstances that placed me at such a unique beginning. I doubt that there's another person on earth who has experienced this kind of youth. I like to think it has provided me with the gift of awareness and appreciation for all things in nature, great and small. It is my wish that my gift is reflected in this photographic representation of the Appalachian Mountains.

Clyde H. Smith